STOURHEAD

Wiltshire

THE NATIONAL TRUST

Acknowledgements

This new guidebook is based on the text of that produced by Dudley Dodd in 1981. The section on the family history has been written by Kenneth Woodbridge. Information about the house derives from numerous sources, the most important being recorded in the bibliography. Special thanks are due to Juliet Allan for information about Flitcroft, to the late Helena Hayward for her research on William and John Linnell, and to John Kenworthy-Browne for his advice about the contents of the house. It also incorporates comments from James Lees-Milne and the late H. P. R. Hoare.

In 1994–5, with the help of a bequest and the generous support of the Hoare family, the Picture Gallery was redecorated and rehung following research by Dudley Dodd and Alastair Laing. The South Apartment was refurnished by the family for their occupation and the Saloon rearranged as an Edwardian drawing-room.

Anthony Mitchell, 1997

Photographs: British Library pp. 15, 19; Courtauld Institute of Art pp. 33, 34, 42, 43 (bottom left); Rick Godley pp. 11, 16, 21 (bottom), 23; *The Ladies' Field* p. 30; National Trust pp. 7, 8 (top), 21 (top), 29 (top), 31, 32, 40; National Trust Photographic Library p. 1; NTPL/Bill Batten front cover, pp. 9, 14, 18, 25; NTPL/John Bethell pp. 8 (bottom), 12 (bottom), 36; NTPL/Prudence Cuming p. 37; NTPL/Angelo Hornak pp. 22, 35, back cover; NTPL/Nick Meers pp. 5, 6, 29 (bottom); NTPL/Kim Oliver p. 41; NTPL/John Hammond pp. 20, 27, 39, 43 (top right), 46; NTPL/Charlie Waite pp. 44, 45.

ISBN 1-84359-031-x

Designed by James Shurmer

Phototypeset in Monotype Bembo Series 270
by SPAN Graphics Ltd, Crawley, West Sussex (SG1003)

Print managed by Centurion Press Ltd (BAS)
for the National Trust (Enterprises) Ltd,
36 Queen Anne's Gate, London SW1H 9AS

(*Front cover*) Detail of a Chippendale armchair in the Library, decorated with an Egyptian head, 1805

(*Title-page*) Stourhead House from the north-east in 1817, before the portico was added; detail from a watercolour by J. C. Buckler

(*Back cover*) The 'Pope's Cabinet' in the Cabinet Room is richly decorated with *pietre dure* and gilt bronze ornaments

CONTENTS

STOURHEAD

HENRY HOARE I

Henry Hoare I purchased old Stourton House in 1717 and swiftly demolished it. He then erected a Palladian villa on an adjacent site and rechristened it Stourhead, dissociating the new Hoare dynasty from the ancient Barons Stourton who had lived there since Saxon times. Henry Hoare I derived his wealth from the bank founded by his father in 1672, which is still a prosperous family business. He appointed as architect for his new house Colen Campbell, leader of the Palladian revival.

HENRY HOARE 'THE MAGNIFICENT'

After his father's death in 1725, Henry Hoare II (nicknamed 'The Magnificent') completed the house, amassing the paintings, sculpture and *objets d'art* which are the nucleus of the present collection. It was he who contrived what is perhaps the most beautiful landscape garden in England, forming the lake in the valley south of the house and building the temples and monuments on its shores.

SIR RICHARD COLT HOARE

In 1783 Henry Hoare II gave the property to his grandson, Sir Richard Colt Hoare, 2nd Bt – known in the family as Colt Hoare. In the history of Stourhead, Colt Hoare plays a prominent role; in the history of Wiltshire he ranks high. Born in 1758, he became a prominent antiquary and scholar and as a county historian he must be regarded as a professional – being author of *The Ancient History of Wiltshire* and *The History of Modern Wiltshire*. He was furthermore a man of taste, an omnivorous collector and patron of the arts. In the 1790s he added the wings, or pavilions, to the house containing the Library and Picture Gallery. His Library is among the most personal and beautiful rooms that have come down to us from Regency times. No less remarkable is the furniture made for the house between 1795 and 1820 by Thomas Chippendale, son of the famous eighteenth-century cabinetmaker.

THE FIRE AND REBUILDING

When Colt Hoare died in 1838, Stourhead passed to his half-brother and ultimately, through cousins, to Sir Henry Hoare, 6th Bt, who inherited in 1894. He brought with him the pick of the contents of Wavendon, the family house in Buckinghamshire which he quit to live at Stourhead. In 1902 fire gutted the centre of the house but left unscathed the Library and Picture Gallery. The outbreak occurred on the second floor and spread slowly through the building so that, by dint of good organisation, the estate staff rescued all but the very largest items from the principal rooms. Faced with the decision as to what to do with the shell, Sir Henry did not waver. The property was fully insured so, recruiting Doran Webb, a local architect, he set about rebuilding the house in replica. Only in the design of the west front, the Saloon and the Staircase Hall did Doran Webb depart significantly from the original, and elsewhere he conformed conscientiously with Colen Campbell. But in 1905, shortly before the work was completed, the main roof-timbers began to sag alarmingly. By this time relations between architect and client had deteriorated so far that Sir Henry dismissed Doran Webb and appointed as his successor Sir Aston Webb (no relation).

Sir Henry's only son died serving in the First World War. One year before his own death in 1947, Sir Henry gave the National Trust the house, Pleasure Grounds and about 3,000 acres of the surrounding estate.

The portico on the east front. The eagles that perch on the stone basins are the emblem of the Hoare family

TOUR OF THE HOUSE

THE CARRIAGE DRIVE

Where the path from the car-park crosses the road stands a great castellated gateway marking the main entrance to Stourhead. It was erected in 1799 by Colt Hoare, who wrote in the Stourhead Annals, 'March, Pulled down a Gateway with two Towers leading from the Village to my Stable Yard. April, began rebuilding them according to the same plan at the foot of the Hill – Completed them before the Winter.' Beside the Gateway is a lodge with exaggerated eaves which was built about the same time to designs of 1793 by Willey Reveley, a pupil of Sir William Chambers.

From the entrance the metalled drive sweeps gently uphill with the park on the right bordered by ancient Spanish chestnut trees. To the left lies the stableyard, probably occupying part of the site of old Stourton House, which Henry Hoare I demolished to make way for his new house.

THE EAST FRONT

Stourhead comprises the villa designed by Colen Campbell and built for Henry Hoare I between 1721 and 1725 with flanking pavilions added by his grandson, Colt Hoare, some 70 years later.

The original house was designed by Campbell in the style deriving from villas built by the sixteenth-century architect Palladio for wealthy Venetians in the neighbourhood of Vicenza. The most striking feature is the pedimented front, like the end of a Greek or Roman temple grafted on to the house. Its main characteristics are plainness and rationality, achieved by using a system of proportion which harmonises all the parts. During the eighteenth century the Palladian villa became the most popular style for English country houses. Stourhead was among the first.

Campbell based the layout and elevation of Stourhead on the villa which Palladio had built in

The east front

The east front, from Colen Campbell's Vitruvius Britannicus, *1725*

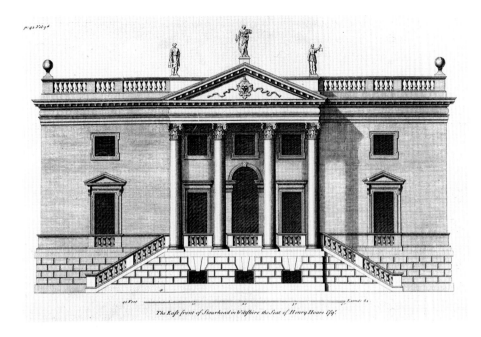

the 1560s for the wealthy foundry owner Leonardo Emo. In deference to the English climate, Campbell planned Stourhead with a massive prostyle (or open) portico; but subsequently, Henry Hoare I abandoned the idea in favour of the engaged frontispiece of pilasters and a triangular pediment, which survived until 1838 (illustrated on p. 1). Nathaniel Ireson was the builder.

In 1792 Colt Hoare virtually tripled the length of the east front by adding the pavilions to house his Library on the south side and Picture Gallery on the north. The work was entrusted to Messrs Moulton & Atkinson of Salisbury and the design was probably Colt Hoare's own. Reticence is the keynote of the new pavilions. As Colt Hoare wrote in his *Modern Wiltshire*: 'The same style of architecture is faithfully kept up; and at this time, though after the short lapse of twenty years, the walls of the new buildings have so completely acquired the tints of the old, that the interval between 1720 and 1820 cannot be distinguished.' The building stone came from the Doulting quarries, near Shepton Mallet in Somerset.

The portico was eventually added by Henry Hugh Hoare, 3rd Bt, in 1838–9 under the supervision of Charles Parker, a pupil of Sir Jeffry Wyatville. In minor but significant details he departed from Campbell's original plans, placing an attic above the pediment, omitting the basement window and adding returns to the twin flights of steps. These were further enhanced by four great stone basins on which perch eagles, the Hoare emblem.

Towards the end of the nineteenth century the sash windows were replaced by casements with unsympathetic plate glass: unfortunately, this error was repeated during the reconstruction after the 1902 fire. At that time the balustrades were added to the pavilions, concealing their shallow hipped roofs, and the three lead statues were moved from the Temple of Apollo in the Pleasure Grounds and set above the portico.

The Interior

The double flights of steps between the stone piers with their eagle basins lead to the state rooms. These, in the correct Palladian tradition derived from the Italian sixteenth-century *palazzi*, are ranged on the *piano nobile* (main floor), which is raised over a semi-basement where the kitchens and offices are situated. Through the great portico the front door leads directly into the Entrance Hall.

7

THE ENTRANCE HALL

The Entrance Hall is a 30-foot cube. Throughout Colen Campbell's original house, the dimensions of the rooms are carefully related to one another: the flanking Music Room and Cabinet Room each measure 30 by 20 feet. Similar proportions occur at Palladio's Palazzo Porto-Colleoni in Vicenza, a building studied by Campbell, who shared Palladio's belief that beauty could be achieved through simple mathematical relationships.

The original decoration was almost totally destroyed in the fire of 1902. Working from photographs and fragments of mouldings, the craftsmen tried to reproduce it, but they were hampered by lack of adequate drawings from the architect Doran Webb so that features such as the capitals of the doorcases are weak versions of the originals. The plaster cornice was remodelled in freehand by a Signor Agostini of Bristol in 1904–5.

The present red and white colour scheme and the green and grey veined marble floor recall the Edwardian era at Stourhead.

(Right)   Charles I; by Hubert le Sueur (Entrance Hall)

PICTURES

(A leaflet is available listing all the pictures in the house in room order.)

OVER CHIMNEYPIECE:

136 SAMUEL WOODFORDE, RA (1763–1817)
Sir Richard Colt Hoare (1758–1838) with his son, Henry, 1795/6
Colt Hoare first grouped the family portraits here, because, as he explained in *Modern Wiltshire*:

They remind us of the genealogy of our families, and recall to our minds the hospitality, &c. of its former inhabitants, and on the first entrance of the friend, or stranger, seem to greet them with a SALVE, or welcome.

UPPER ROW, OPPOSITE FRONT DOOR:

115 MICHAEL DAHL (1656/9–1743)
Henry Hoare I (1677–1725)
He holds a drawing of the elevation of the house in his hand.

OPPOSITE CHIMNEYPIECE:

156 MICHAEL DAHL (1656/9–1743) and JOHN WOOTTON (*c.*1682–1756)
Henry Hoare II (1705–85)
The creator of the Pleasure Grounds on horseback. Dahl painted the figure, Wootton the horse. Horace Walpole described it as 'large as life and good'.

ON EITHER SIDE:

160–1 ST GEORGE HARE (1856–1933)
Sir Henry Hoare, 6th Bt (1865–1947) and Lady Hoare (d.1947)
Sir Henry restored the house after the fire and gave it to the National Trust in 1946.

SCULPTURE

BELOW EQUESTRIAN PORTRAIT:

HUBERT LE SUEUR (active 1610–43)
Charles I (1600–49)
Le Sueur is best known for his equestrian statue of Charles I in Trafalgar Square, but this much-repro-

duced image of the king helped to popularise the portrait bust. This cast was sold from Whitehall Palace in 1650 and was first recorded at Stourhead in the mid-eighteenth century.

FURNITURE

FLANKING DOOR TO INNER HALL:

Pair of console tables with fox supports, made in the 1740s for the Little Dining Room, probably to a design by Henry Flitcroft.

Late eighteenth-century hall-chairs with caned seats and wheelbacks centring on marquetry panels with the Hoare crest.

Four bronzed torchères, carved with tigers' heads, made in 1802 by Thomas Chippendale the Younger for the Picture Gallery Ante-Room.

THE INNER HALL

In place of the original single staircase destroyed by the fire, Doran Webb installed twin flights and galleries. The idea was taken from the much larger entrance hall of the mid-seventeenth century Coleshill in Berkshire (itself destroyed by fire in 1952) and is very cramped here; worse still, the stairs were made narrow and dangerously steep.

FURNITURE

Two late eighteenth-century hall-chairs, en suite with those in the Entrance Hall.

Pair of two rococo pier-glasses, probably those made by John Linnell in 1753 as the focal point of the drawing-room at Barn Elms, the Surrey home of Colt Hoare's father.

The early eighteenth-century burr walnut longcase clock has a movement by Andrew Dunlop of London.

The settee has a scallop-shell cresting in William Kent's style of the 1730s.

PICTURES

The passage on the right contains two watercolours of rooms at Wavendon showing furniture now at Stourhead. The first-floor landing was designed for displaying four large paintings rescued from the Saloon during the fire in 1902 (see picture list).

SCULPTURE

AT FOOT OF STAIRS:

JOHN MICHAEL RYSBRACK (1694–1770)
A group of framed plaster reliefs
Three were purchased by Henry Hoare II at the sculptor's sale in 1767.

Return to the Entrance Hall, turn right and pass through the Music Room and Library Ante-Room into the Library.

THE LIBRARY

This is one of the finest surviving Regency libraries in Britain and miraculously escaped the fire in 1902. It was built in 1792 by Messrs Moulton & Atkinson of Salisbury for Colt Hoare, who was probably closely involved in its design. It has been called 'probably Colt Hoare's supreme achievement as a patron, as complete in conception as his grandfather's garden; and it represents the introverted way of life he found in the Italian monasteries without any of the attendant disadvantages.'

LUNETTES

At the far end of the room is a painted window by Francis Eginton after Raphael's famous Vatican fresco of *The School of Athens*, which depicts the greatest thinkers of the Classical world. The lunette at the inner end of the room was painted on canvas by Colt Hoare's favourite British artist, Samuel Woodforde, after Raphael's *Parnassus* from the same cycle, which shows Apollo and the Nine Muses, symbols of artistic creativity. Colt Hoare clearly thought that they would help to inspire his own work as historian and topographer.

CEILING AND CARPET

The lattice-work on the barrel ceiling, repainted following the original in 1962, reflects the carpet, whose pattern of interlacing motifs derives from a Roman tiled pavement. The present carpet was woven in 1968 at the Wilton Royal Carpet Factory and reproduces the Brussels carpet installed in 1852, itself a replica of the original.

CHIMNEYPIECE AND OVERMANTEL

The present marble chimneypiece and plaster overmantel were brought from Wavendon in 1913. The latter dates from the 1720s and contains a gesso

The Library

relief depicting the Old Testament story of *Tobit lending money to Gabael*. Tobit was later blinded by sparrows' droppings and sent out his son Tobias to recover the loan, when he encountered the Archangel Raphael – a much more frequent subject for artists. It is a preliminary model for the marble relief made by Pierre Legros *c.*1702 for the chapel of Monte di Pietà in Rome.

BOOKS

Colt Hoare assembled a vast library of rare volumes on the history and topography of Britain, largely to provide source material for his scholarly publications, *The Ancient History of Wiltshire* (1810–21) and *The History of Modern Wiltshire* (1822–44). Unfortunately, Colt Hoare's books were sold in 1883, and the Library today is a miscellany from Wavendon and Oxenham (the family estate in Devon), with some of Colt Hoare's manuscripts and travel journals. His archaeological collection is now in the Devizes Museum.

In the present century, Alda, Lady Hoare collected the works of Thomas Hardy, who became a family friend, and of other authors she admired. A photograph of Hardy is displayed on the centre table.

The Library in 1901

SCULPTURE

ON LARGE LIBRARY DESK:

Terracotta model of Hercules, made by Rysbrack in 1744, before Henry Hoare II commissioned the large marble statue in the Pantheon, completed in 1756. Rysbrack left the model to Henry in his will in 1770.

IN NICHES ABOVE DOORS:

Marble busts of John Milton as a youth and as an old man, by Rysbrack. Commissioned *c.*1740 by William Benson, from whom they passed to his nephew, Henry Hoare II. Busts of famous writers were a favourite decoration for country-house libraries.

PICTURES

ON FAR WINDOW WALL:

COPLESTONE WARRE BAMPFYLDE (1720–91)
Stourhead Pleasure Grounds
Views to the Pantheon and to the Bristol Cross, c. 1775
A pair of watercolours by a friend of Henry Hoare II often at Stourhead.

The Chippendale writing-desk is carved with the heads of Egyptians and classical philosophers

ON EASEL BELOW BUST OF YOUNG MILTON:

A watercolour by Francis Nicholson (1753–1844) records the appearance of the Library in Colt Hoare's time. It shows the furniture still in the room, as well as the upholstery and tablecloths, which have long since perished.

FURNITURE

The Library furniture was supplied in 1804–5 by Thomas Chippendale the Younger, who refurnished the house for Colt Hoare between 1795 and 1820, as well as equipping the new Library and Picture Gallery. Chippendale went bankrupt in 1804, and it was thanks to the loyalty of a few clients like Colt Hoare that he managed to rebuild the business and continue until his death in 1822.

The large library steps and the centre-table opposite, decorated with Egyptian heads, were invoiced for in 1804 at £52 and £21 respectively.

The massive writing-desk has legs carved with the heads of philosophers and Egyptians, and was designed to be taken to pieces. It was supplied by Chippendale in 1805 for £115.

The set of armchairs and the large portfolio stand were also supplied in 1805. With their round seats and yoke-shaped backs, the chairs recall traditional eighteenth-century French patterns for desk chairs. Indeed the Library furniture is more French in style than pieces Chippendale had previously supplied to Stourhead, and suggests that he visited Paris during the Peace of Amiens (1802–3), and was aware of chairs made by the Jacob frères around 1800. The chairs also have Egyptian heads with the *nemes* or *klaft* head-dress, first introduced after Napoleon's campaign of 1797–8.

THE LIBRARY ANTE-ROOM

This unobtrusively connects Colt Hoare's Regency Library with Colen Campbell's house of the 1720s.

PICTURES

It is hung with watercolours from Colt Hoare's collection, notably, on the window wall, a pair by J. R. Cozens and Italian scenes by John 'Warwick' Smith (1749–1831), who taught him sketching.

High on the wall opposite is a huge panoramic view of *Stourhead Lake* attributed to Francis Nicholson, showing Colt Hoare's planting in about 1816, when it was approaching maturity.

SCULPTURE

The left-hand bust is of Colt Hoare in later life by R. C. Lucas (1800–83), who carved his monument in Salisbury Cathedral, next to his portrait as a younger man.

The right-hand bust is of King Alfred, carved in 1764 by Rysbrack, when the sculptor was 70.

FURNITURE

The early eighteenth-century walnut longcase clock has a movement by Henry Massy of London.

The two low banquettes, or 'sofa seats', were supplied by Chippendale in 1802 (the upholstery is modern).

THE MUSIC ROOM

The name of the room dates back to the eighteenth century, when Henry Hoare II installed a chamber organ in the niche opposite the fireplace, but unfortunately it perished in the 1902 fire.

CHIMNEYPIECE

The chimneypiece in the style of William Kent (1685/6–1748), with chin-stroking flanking figures, was remade after the fire. The overmantel, *c*.1740, frames the painting of *The Interior of St Peter's at Rome* (196) after Giovanni Panini (1691–1765).

PICTURES

With one or two exceptions, the pictures are those acquired for the room by Colt Hoare, who commended them in *Modern Wiltshire* as 'a pleasing selection of fancy pictures, by modern Artists of the British School, and such as both now and hereafter will do credit to them'. In contrast to his grandfather, he displayed greater enthusiasm as a patron of contemporary artists than as a collector of Old Masters.

Prominent on the west wall is *Diana and Actaeon* (189) by Sir Augustus Wall Callcott with figures by William Owen. This painting was exhibited at the Royal Academy in 1810 but failed to find a buyer until purchased by Colt Hoare in the following year. *A Shepherdess with a Lamb in a Storm* (192) by Samuel Woodforde and *A Girl deploring the Death*

The Music Room

of a *Pheasant* (186) by Henry Thomson reveal an unexpectedly sentimental streak in him – a reminder that such 'fancy' pictures, brimming with bucolic sentiment, were very fashionable at that time.

FURNITURE

The set of chairs and the pair of low cabinets 'with scrowl heads' were supplied by Chippendale for this room in 1812. The design of the chairs derives from the single chairs made for the Library in 1805. The armchairs are *en suite* and resemble traditional *bergères* (wide armchairs with rounded backs) without the usual upholstery. The mahogany is shown off to advantage by the gilding and the gilt-brass moulding, in the manner of contemporary French furniture.

IN NICHE OPPOSITE FIREPLACE:

A gilt side-table, c.1730, in the manner of William Kent. The top is carved with the arms of Susanna Colt, second wife of Henry Hoare II.

The square piano is by Christopher Ganer, 1784.

THE LITTLE DINING ROOM

This became known as the Little Dining Room in Victorian times, to distinguish it from the Saloon, which by then was also being used as a dining-room.

It probably began life as a garden hall, providing access to the south lawn outside down twin flights of steps. The great Venetian window then formed the focal point of the south façade. But when Colt Hoare added the Library wing in 1792, he removed the door to the garden and the steps, which drew attention to the fractured symmetry of this façade. Between 1802 and 1809 he renovated the room and bought new furniture from Chippendale.

After the fire, the room was carefully reconstructed: the decorative ceiling was recast by Signor Agostini at a cost of £105, and the stone columns were all renewed.

CHIMNEYPIECE

This is a copy of the one probably brought from Wavendon in 1895.

PICTURES

'In this apartment we are gratified with the sight of some very fine specimens of painting in crayons, a style now quite unfashionable.' Thus Colt Hoare described the Dining Room pictures in *Modern Wiltshire*. Today pastels still predominate, notwithstanding the pictures brought from Wavendon. These include:

OVERMANTEL:

A Hunting Picture with Henry Hoare II and his uncle Benjamin in 1729 (250) by John Wootton (*c*.1682–1756).

ON EITHER SIDE:

Three pastel portraits by Francis Cotes (1725–70).

Sir Richard Hoare, 1st Baronet (left), who married his cousin Anne (right), the daughter of Henry Hoare II. They were the parents of Colt Hoare. Below Sir Richard is his second wife, Frances Ann Acland, with a spinning wheel (248).

The other pastels are by William Hoare of Bath (1707–92), who was no relation of the family, but a friend of Henry Hoare. William Hoare's daughter Mary, also an artist, married Henry Hoare of Beckenham.

The Little Dining Room in 1824; a sketch by J. C. Buckler (British Library)

The Little Dining Room

OVER DOOR TO SOUTH APARTMENT:

The Nymph of the Grot
The sculpture of Ariadne in the grotto at Stourhead. Given by Hoare of Bath to Henry Hoare II in 1760 in gratitude for these commissions.

SILVER

ON MAHOGANY SIDEBOARD:

The great silver gilt dish was made by Heinrich Mannlich in the late seventeenth century in Augsburg, the centre of the European goldsmiths' trade.

It depicts *The Death of Cyrus at the hands of Queen Tomyris* (taken from an engraving after a painting by Rubens). It was given to Colt Hoare's grandfather, Sir Richard Hoare, when Lord Mayor of London in 1745.

The partly gilt stand, with two spritely beasts as supporters, is tentatively attributed to the carver and sculptor Sefferin Alken, who received commissions from the family between 1745 and 1783.

ON CENTRE-TABLE:

A seventeenth-century German silver gilt and agate centrepiece in the form of a double-headed eagle, the Hoares' emblem.

ON SIDE–TABLE BETWEEN COLUMNS:

The silver bears the arms of Hoare impaling Acland, commemorating the marriage of Sir Richard Hoare of Barn Elms to his second wife, Francis Ann Acland, in 1761. The plates and tureen have been kindly lent by Hoare's Bank.

The large salver, hallmarked John Carter 1772, was acquired with the help of the National Art Collections Fund.

FURNITURE

The mahogany sideboard, carved with leopards' heads and lion's paw feet, was supplied by Chippendale in 1802.

The large oval wine-cooler, decorated with marquetry medallions and festoons, may have been that bought from a Mr Ward in 1779.

The mahogany dining-table and the smaller sideboard (fitted with the customary cupboard for a chamber-pot so that gentlemen could relieve themselves) were also made by Chippendale.

The set of mid-eighteenth-century walnut chairs with open-work backs in the form of shells may be that bought by Henry Hoare II from Giles Grendey in 1746.

THE SOUTH APARTMENT

The first room, the South Room, has recently been arranged by the Hoare family as a private sitting-room. Over the chimneypiece is John Wootton's *The Bloody-shouldered Arabian*, which hung here in the late Sir Henry's time. On the right hangs an elegant pastel portrait of Lady Hoare by Augusto Stoppoloni. In the break-front bookcase opposite is a group of Chelsea-Derby porcelain.

Beyond is a small room which is hung with a portrait of Henry (1784–1836), only son of Colt Hoare, as a boy, by Woodforde, and paintings and lithographs by Yeend King and Théophile Steinlen (1859–1923), acquired by Sir Henry and his wife, Alda.

FURNITURE

Pair of two caned-back mahogany chairs, supplied in 1816 by Chippendale, who described them as 'Hunting Chairs'.

THE SALOON

According to Colt Hoare, the room was originally intended as a chapel and it was called this on Colen Campbell's plan. About 1744, however, Henry Hoare II commissioned Henry Flitcroft to convert it to a saloon, because by then a grand reception room for county balls, theatricals, concerts and other entertainments had become essential to all country houses of consequence. Flitcroft extended the room by 15 feet, rebuilding the central bays of the west front in the process. Loyal to the tradition of Colen Campbell, he designed an interior of restrained opulence where, in Colt Hoare's words, 'regard has been paid to just proportions in every appendage subordinate to the general proportions of length, breadth and height, which are also true, being 45 by 30'. Something of its splendour is apparent from J. C. Buckler's drawing of 1824 (illustrated on p. 19).

During the fire the furniture and smaller paintings were snatched to safety but the three largest canvases perished, along with all the carving and decorations.

In 1902 Doran Webb seems to have been given a free hand in redesigning the room. He lowered the ceiling (fitting in two bedrooms above), extended the room further westwards and introduced the screen of columns, an idea borrowed from the Little Dining Room. The massive plaster cornice is imitation Flitcroft but the ill-matched compartment ceiling is 'Wrenaissance'. The red flock wallpaper was put up by the Trust in the 1950s; in recent years it has been sprayed a more sombre colour.

Sir Aston Webb designed the flight of steps from the central window, which looks out over the parkland and the obelisk erected by Henry Hoare in 1746 and rebuilt in Bath stone in 1839.

CHIMNEYPIECE

The late eighteenth-century chimneypiece and overmantel were moved from Wavendon and installed first in the Library, and later here. The frieze is decorated with little plaques after Flaxman. It is not known who carved the overmantel, but the picture within is by Angelica Kauffman (1741–1807).

PICTURES

After the fire Sir Henry installed family portraits in what was a large dining-room – a role since fulfilled for many years by the Column Room. As the

The Saloon

Saloon is essentially Edwardian in character, rather than Palladian, it has now been arranged with the help of the Hoare family as a drawing-room, inspired by the photographs of other rooms in the house during Alda's reign, and is occasionally used by the family. After the fire, Sir Henry and Lady Hoare were keen patrons of St George Hare, whose 'fancy' pictures were exhibited at the Royal Acad-

emy and whose self-portrait hangs on the right of the window wall. Formerly scattered about the house and then banished to the attics, they now once again enrich the collection.

FLANKING FAR DOOR TO INNER HALL:

Full-length portraits of Harry Hoare in 1909 aged 21, who was to die of wounds in the First World War at Alexandria in 1917, and of his mother Alda, Lady Hoare, in 1910; by St George Hare (1857–1933).

The Saloon in 1824; a sketch by J. C. Buckler (British Library)

SCULPTURE

The marble busts in the far corners are eighteenth-century Roman copies of the antique *Vestal Virgin* (Farnese Collection, now at Naples) and the *Zingara* or *Gypsy* (Villa Borghese, Rome), and may have been acquired by Colt Hoare on the Grand Tour.

FURNITURE

Among pieces from various eighteenth-century suites of seat furniture are:

RIGHT OF FAR DOOR:

A marquetry commode c.1760.

RIGHT OF FIREPLACE:

A bonheur-du-jour (lady's writing-table) in the French style, probably by John Linnell *c.*1780. The marquetry door panels representing nymphs playing musical instruments are tentatively attributed to the Swedish émigré cabinetmaker Christopher Fürloh.

Pair of little satinwood 'Oval Claw Work tables' supplied by Chippendale.

CARPET

The splendid Axminster carpet is described in the 1838 inventory and sketchily depicted by Buckler.

THE COLUMN ROOM

At the time of Horace Walpole's visit in July 1762 it was the 'bedchamber with columns'.

PICTURES

OVERMANTEL:

Architectural Capriccio by Francis Harding (active 1745–67) in the manner of Panini.

In Colt Hoare's time this room became a temple to the watercolour. It is still hung with views of Rome and the surrounding countryside by the Swiss artist Abraham-Louis Ducros (1748–1810), much favoured by Colt Hoare, who declared that Ducros painted watercolours like oil paintings and influenced the English watercolour school. Colt also patronised Turner, whose early watercolours of Salisbury Cathedral, sold in 1883, also hung here; some are now in the British Museum and the

Salisbury Museum. Stonehenge and Malmesbury Abbey reflect his antiquarian and topographical tastes.

THE ITALIAN ROOM

Henry Hoare II conceived the room as a state bedroom, although by the 1720s the convention of reserving a bed for visiting royalty was moribund. When Colt Hoare came to live at Stourhead, he made it his own bedroom, installing a 'single screwed four post Bedstead [with] Mahogany feet pillars and Chintz Furniture'. Subsequently, it became a parlour and by the 1880s it was being referred to as the Italian Room – an allusion perhaps to the coloured engravings after Old Masters first recorded here in Colt Hoare's time and to the painted ceiling (then attributed to Italian artists), which was destroyed in the fire, with the rest of the decoration.

As befits a Palladian house, certain architectural motifs recur and indeed they dominate the Italian Room, where the Venetian window is echoed by the rib-vaulted alcove opposite (originally filled by a bed). In 1762 Walpole commended this 'bed-chamber with a painted alcove' as 'pretty taste'. Both alcove and ceiling were decorated with medallions and delicate interlacing scrolls painted in the mid-eighteenth-century style. This is recorded in a photograph taken shortly before the fire destroyed the interior. When reconstructing the room, Doran Webb copied the architectural elements but he did not reproduce the painted decoration. The new plasterwork has the tell-tale doughy quality characteristic of Signor Agostini's work.

CHIMNEYPIECE

The pretty mid-eighteenth-century marble chimneypiece with a plaque representing *The Marriage of Cupid and Psyche* was brought from Wavendon in 1913.

*(Left)   The Stables of
the Villa Maecenas at
Tivoli; watercolour by
Abraham-Louis Ducros
(Column Room)*

*(Right)   The Italian
Room in 1901*

The Italian Room

OVERMANTEL:

The Sacrifice of Iphigenia, with figures by Jacopo Amigoni (1682?–1752) and capriccio of antique Rome and Glanum (now St Rémy) by Francis Harding (active 1745–67) in the manner of Panini.

IN ALCOVE:

A group of nine copies of Old Masters in sepia by James Rouby (1750–1812).

FURNITURE

The seat furniture is from the large eighteenth-century mahogany set that was in the old Saloon in 1824 where it can be seen under case covers in Buckler's sketch (illustrated on p. 19). The settee from this set is now in the Picture Gallery.

The mahogany card-table, carved with bacchic masks and lion's paw feet, was made in 1740 by William Linnell for Sir Richard Hoare (brother of Henry Hoare II) when he lived at Blackheath.

The four walnut chests-of-drawers with folding tops for writing date from about 1710. Because such pieces were useful in small bedrooms, they are often described as bachelor chests.

IN ALCOVE OPPOSITE CHIMNEYPIECE:

A Palladian mirror in the style of William Kent.

THE CABINET ROOM

In pride of place is the monumental Florentine cabinet acquired by Henry Hoare II in 1741–2 (see below). Around it he hung paintings by Canaletto, Maratta, Nicolas Poussin and copies after Raphael. Having completed the Picture Gallery in 1802, Colt Hoare rearranged the pictures at Stourhead, gathering to the Cabinet Room his favourite landscapes, including *Lake Avernus with Aeneas and the Cumaean Sibyl*, painted by Turner in 1815 after a sketch by Colt Hoare himself, and now in America. It is now once again close-hung with landscapes, eg by Orizzonte, Zuccarelli, Richard Wilson and Henry Hoare's friend C.W. Bampfylde, and with a group of small paintings by Lagrenée acquired by Henry Hoare.

DECORATION

Colt Hoare refurnished the room in 1802. The textiles he purchased have long since perished and are known only from Chippendale's accounts: a

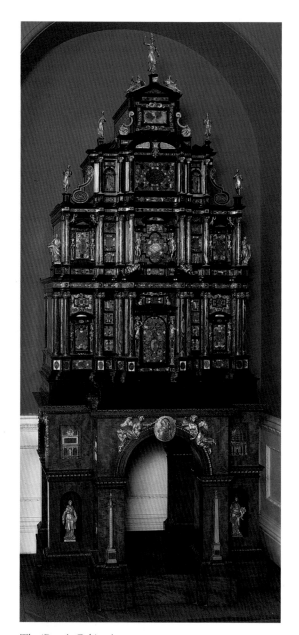

The 'Pope's Cabinet'

(Right) The Cabinet Room

green serge floor cloth, 'blue Rosette callico' cushion covers, a window curtain of 'blue Sattin with black spots', a pair of footstools in red Morocco leather and, most sumptuous of all, a drapery for the alcove of 'Rich blue velvet' with gold fringe and tassels.

Today the room is painted in Alda Hoare's red and white livery. The green Donegal carpet was bought recently.

CHIMNEYPIECE

The white marble chimneypiece was moved from the South Apartment after the fire.

THE 'POPE'S CABINET'

Such luxury cabinets were conceived with elaborate Mannerist façades of ebony and gilt bronze, which served as a frame to show off one of the most spectacular and costly products of the Ducal Workshops in Florence. This was the *pietre dure* (literally 'hard stones') inlay, an immensely time-consuming technique of marquetry using different coloured pieces of highly polished marble, porphyry, jasper and other rich materials. The cabinets were intended to contain, though not to display, collections of gems, cameos, medals and other precious objects.

The story goes that the cabinet once belonged to Pope Sixtus V (hence the name) and then passed to his brother's family, the Perettis, the last of whom, being a nun, left it to a convent in Rome, where it was purchased by Henry Hoare II. But stylistic evidence suggests that it was made in the mid-seventeenth century and is contemporary with the *pietre dure* cabinet or *stippone*, once in the Uffizi in

Florence, which bears the arms of Grand Duke Ferdinand II of Tuscany, who reigned from 1621 to 1670. If so, it could not have belonged to Sixtus V, who died in 1590. However, Henry Hoare II believed the provenance and commissioned Mr Boson to make an elaborate mahogany stand with carved reliefs commemorating the Pope's architectural achievements in Rome. Colt Hoare later commissioned Chippendale to make an ornate gilt cornice for the niche curtain 'finished in Burnished Gold with the Popes tiara and other insignias'. Partly concealed by the blue velvet curtain (also supplied by Chippendale), the cabinet would then have gleamed in the semi-darkness like some great shrouded reliquary.

During the fire, the cabinet and stand were carried to safety but the gilt cornice perished together with other fittings in the room.

OTHER FURNITURE

Six from a set of eight satinwood and ebony armchairs made for the room by Chippendale and invoiced in 1802 (two are missing). Their design derives from chairs made by the great Parisian *menuisier* (chair-maker) Georges Jacob in the late eighteenth century.

Pair of satinwood pole-screens supplied by Chippendale in 1802.

The stools were made by Chippendale in 1804, when Colt Hoare had a bad attack of gout.

The oval inlaid satinwood rent-table of about 1780 came from the library at Wavendon.

SCULPTURE

SILHOUETTED AGAINST EAST WINDOW:

An unusually large eighteenth-century vase made of bluejohn, a form of fluorspar quarried in Derbyshire.

THE PICTURE GALLERY
ANTE-ROOM

To herald the Picture Gallery, Colt Hoare arrayed this room in considerable splendour. The walls were close-hung with Old Master paintings and the carpet was *en suite* with the Cabinet Room and Picture Gallery.

FURNITURE

Two of the four 'sofa seats' supplied by Chippendale remain here.

Pair of rosewood elbow chairs, by Chippendale, 1802. The sets in the Cabinet Room and the Saloon were made later that year to the same design.

THE PICTURE GALLERY

In the Picture Gallery Colt Hoare brought together the pick of his grandfather's picture collection and of the Old Masters and contemporary paintings which he himself acquired. Completed in 1802, the room escaped damage in the fire and survives, with minor changes, as an example of Regency taste. It occupies the entire north pavilion above the semi-basement (where Colt Hoare had an archaeological museum) and is lit by two rows of east-facing windows, which cast a cool, rather uneven light after the morning sun has moved around the house.

The Gallery was intended as a formal room where shutters were closed and furniture shrouded in case covers (supplied by Chippendale) except when Colt Hoare was showing the collection. By the end of the nineteenth century, however, Sir Henry and Lady Hoare were rearranging the Gallery as a drawing-room, fitting much-needed radiators (now concealed) and filling up the floor space with spare furniture from Wavendon. The 1901 photographs show the Gallery submerging in a rising tide of chairs, settees, occasional tables and pot plants.

DECORATION

The decoration is simple with a plain ceiling, architectural cornice and green walls. Chippendale supplied the original furnishings including a fitted Brussels carpet, 'Yellow and black Star sattin' curtains and chair cushions in 'Yellow Star callico', all of which have long since disappeared. The yellow and black textiles, the satinwood and ebony furniture and the walls massed with gilt picture frames would have made a dazzling scheme, although Colt Hoare does not tell us the colour of either the walls or the carpet.

The Picture Gallery has been redecorated several times, notably with a red cabbage wallpaper in the 1890s and a green striped paper in 1960. The latter had faded and was damaged by the leaking roof, so in 1994 the walls were repainted green to match surviving fragments of paint.

The Picture Gallery

CARPET

A new wall-to-wall Brussels worsted carpet was woven in 1994 by the firm of Woodward Grosvenor to a design of 1827 found in their Kidderminster archives.

CHIMNEYPIECE

The white marble chimneypiece, installed in 1801, has a bas-relief representing *The Education of Bacchus*, copied from an antique vase used as a font at Gaeta di Mola, which Colt Hoare saw in Italy.

PICTURES

The pictures have recently been rehung closer to Colt Hoare's original intention, which was to emulate those picture galleries he had seen in Italian *palazzi*. The larger canvases are raised above a predella (lower part of an altarpiece) of choice small paintings to be enjoyed at eye level in highly carved frames, a principle that can be seen in the photographs of 1901. The loss of sixteen paintings (from the Gallery alone) in the heirloom sale of 1883 had been compensated for by the 6th Baronet's introduction of paintings from Wavendon a few years before. *Country Life* in 1951 still records the survival of this idea, but the Trust thinned out the pictures at the end of that decade in favour of an elegant, simpler presentation of masterpieces, before recent research on the history of collections and picture hanging made these subjects better understood. Surprisingly, the shadow of Colt Hoare's original early nineteenth-century hang was still to be seen on the old plaster when the modern wallpaper was removed (suggesting that the walls were, perhaps, originally papered). The paintings from Wavendon, introduced in the 1890s, include, significantly, the splendid pair of landscapes by Gaspard Dughet (Nicolas Poussin's brother-in-law) originally acquired for Henry Hoare in 1758, but never previously at Stourhead, and later inherited by the 6th Baronet. Colt Hoare would never have mixed landscapes with Old Masters, but these, together with the two sizeable copies of Claudes in the Palazzo Doria in Rome, now on the south (entrance) wall, are typical of his grandfather's taste.

The Gallery has always been dominated by three mighty canvases. The two flanking the chimneypiece were acquired by Henry Hoare II:

LEFT OF CHIMNEYPIECE:

16 CARLO MARATTA (1625–1713)
Marchese Pallavicini and the Artist, 1705
The picture celebrates Pallavicini's achievements as a patron of the arts. Bought from the Arnaldi collection for Henry Hoare in 1758 by Horace Mann, the British representative in Florence.

RIGHT OF CHIMNEYPIECE:

17 ANTON RAPHAEL MENGS (1728–79)
Caesar and Cleopatra
Commissioned from the artist by Henry Hoare in 1759 as a companion to the Maratta, this is an early sign of the Neo-classical revival. The unadorned severity of the Doric columns is intended to suggest the noble simplicity of Caesar. The table with the crown is an exact copy of a Roman one, and appeared 50 years later in Thomas Hope's *Household Furniture and Decoration*.

OVERMANTEL:

18 LUDOVICO CARDI (CIGOLI) (1559–1613)
The Adoration of the Magi
This masterpiece was commissioned in 1605 for the Albizzi chapel, San Pietro Maggiore, Florence, and acquired by Colt Hoare in 1790, shortly after the demolition of the church. The spectacular frame is a de luxe version of the standard 'Carlo Maratta' frame, surmounted by a massive ram's head carved

by Chippendale in 1802. The frames throughout the collection are of unusual quality.

Henry Hoare II also bought the work of contemporary Italian artists such as Sebastiano Ricci, Conca and Imperiali, who was responsible for the two large paintings, *The Sacrifice of Noah* (41) and *Rachel sitting on the Household Gods* (42), readily identifiable on the end wall by their ornate rococo frames.

Colt Hoare was also a patron of contemporary artists in England, such as Henry Thomson (1773–1843), whose large paintings, *Distress by Land* (56) and *Distress by Sea* (57), dominate the window wall.

ON ENTRANCE WALL:

21 NICOLAS POUSSIN (1594–1665)
The Choice of Hercules
Hercules chooses between Vice and Virtue, symbolised by two women. Bought from the Duke of Chandos's sale in 1747.

FURNITURE

When it came to equipping the Picture Gallery, potentially the grandest room in the house, Colt Hoare ordered chaste Neo-classical furniture, ungilded (except for the torchères and the curtain cornices) and relying for effect upon the quality of the wood, the design and the craftsmanship. Conforming with the tastes of the day, the proportions are attenuated, a feature emphasised by the ebony and satinwood banding. As with *Directoire* furniture, Chippendale's pieces have very little carved ornament to interrupt their line, and there are no marquetry panels to distract from the natural figure in the wood, which is then shown off to advantage in chair backs and on table tops.

The set of open armchairs is a refined version of those already seen in the house, and described in Chippendale's account of 1802 together with the two 'Unique large Rosewood Sofa tables'.

Chippendale's '2 Very large Black Rose wood horse fire Screens'. Chippendale's repeated references to the size of the furniture may conceal an anxiety as to how it would 'tell' in such a large room. The loss of four settees and two *bergères* which he supplied has certainly unbalanced the gallery, but four *bergères* now at the end of the room are *en suite* with the

(Right) Marchese Pallavicini and the Artist; by Carlo Maratta, 1705 (Picture Gallery)

elbow chairs. There is nothing lightweight about his curtain cornices and the three jardinières in the shape of sarcophagi in the windows.

Two of the giltwood torchères with heavy triangular bases, which are said to have come from Fonthill, were slightly altered by Chippendale and a third was made to match.

The ebb and flow of furniture since the 1890s has left the Gallery with important furniture beside the Chippendale pieces:

ON FAR WALL:

A spectacular English commode dating from about 1785 and of unknown provenance. Harewood predominates as its surface veneer but the two medallions of veiled mourning figures *en grisaille* are framed in broad surrounds of satinwood, and the sides have large satinwood ovals inlaid with musical instruments.

nineteenth century a large conservatory was built on to the south-west end of the house, parallel with the Library. The ground in between was laid out as a formal garden with a fountain erected in the centre in 1860. Sir Henry Hoare, 6th Bt, demolished the conservatory in 1895–6, levelling the site to make way for the terrace built to Doran Webb's design in 1897. After the fire he extended the south façade westward with another two bays rising the full height of the house.

The original walled garden shown on the 1722 estate plan was replaced before 1785 by an extensive lawn flanked by rows of beech trees, but with the axis still determined by the symmetrical façade of Campbell's south front. The south end of the axis was marked by a statue of Apollo on a mount. Colt Hoare removed the statue and softened the avenue effect by planting more trees so that the garden then began to take on its present appearance.

The Exterior

THE SOUTH FRONT

A footpath from the garden entrance beside the stable gates leads through banks of rhododendrons to the south lawn where the house again comes into view.

The south front today is proof of the rather *ad hoc* way in which each generation of the Hoare family has altered the house. Although partly concealed by the Library pavilion, Campbell's original façade can still be discerned. His design, published in the third volume of *Vitruvius Britannicus*, was an eight-bay elevation with a rustic or semi-basement, and two floors above and with a flat roofline enriched by a balustrade, urns and ball finials – rather like the south front of Wilton, which Campbell admired, but without its tall end bays. Decoration is concentrated on the *piano nobile*. The central Venetian window with cartouche above is flanked by windows with surrounds derived from Palladio's Palazzo Thiene in Vicenza.

The balance of the façade was upset when Flitcroft extended the west front in the 1740s. But its symmetry was brutally disrupted in 1792 when Colt Hoare added the Library, jutting out from the original façade and obliterating two bays. In the

THE WEST FRONT

Campbell's original west front was altered by Flitcroft in the 1740s, when he built the magnificent Saloon for Henry Hoare II. To accommodate this, Flitcroft added a projecting centre bay with a Venetian window in the *piano nobile* and a triangular pediment at roof level. This frontispiece, whose proportions and restrained embellishment harmonised with Campbell's work, is seen in the photographs taken in 1902 (illustrated on p. 29).

After the fire Doran Webb was asked to redesign this façade, incorporating additional bedrooms, a bathroom and various service rooms. Latching on to the Palladian style, half remembered and imperfectly understood, he concocted a façade in the classical idiom which must be considered an aberration.

Later Aston Webb designed the flight of steps leading up to the Saloon door decorated by four lead statues moved from the Temple of Apollo in the Pleasure Grounds. He also added balustrades to the screen above; their undulating profile lends a baroque smirk to this unsympathetic façade.

The single-storey extension on the north (left) side of the house was probably built by Henry Hoare II for his expanding collection of paintings. In Colt Hoare's day it was known as the Justice Room and, after the fire, it was refurnished as a billiard-room.

The west front on the morning after the fire in 1902

The west front as rebuilt by Doran Webb

The Picture Gallery in 1901

STOURHEAD AND ITS OWNERS

And happy he, who in a Country Seat,
From Storms of Bus'ness finds a safe Retreat . . .
Where all around delightful Landskips lie,
And pleasing Prospects entertain his Eye.

René Rapin, *Of Gardens*, translated by James Gardiner, 1706

Stourhead was created in the eighteenth century by the banking family of Hoare. The generations of portraits hanging on the walls were a witness to their continuity, as were the funerary monuments in the church, tokens of immortality more durable than flesh. Those of the founding Hoares of Stourhead dominate the south aisle; elsewhere the effigy of a lady, *c*.1400, and the recumbent effigies of the 6th Lord Stourton and his wife recall a more ancient family whose arms, '*sable, a bend or, between six fountains*', still announce that for over 700 years they were lords of the springs of the River Stour, in the valley still known as Six Wells Bottom.

THE STOURTON FAMILY

Whether or not it was on Stourton soil that Alfred the Great set up his standard before marching to defeat the Danes at Edington, it is certain the Stourtons were a family of local consequence in Saxon times. Botolph de la Stourton (pronounced *Sterton*) married a daughter of Godwin, first earl of the West Saxons. His son Robert received a licence to build Stourton House, which Leland described in the mid-sixteenth century as having two courtyards, 'the fronte of the ynner courte is magnificent, and high embatelid castelle lyke'. For John Aubrey, visiting over a century later, the house evoked 'the time of the old English Barons . . . Here is a great open-roofed hall, and an extraordinary large and high open-rooftd kitchen'. These descriptions and a sketch by Aubrey (illustrated below) are all that remain of the medieval pile pulled down by Henry Hoare I in 1718.

Successive members of the family were returned to Parliament. Sir William Stourton represented Somerset in 1399, and was elected Speaker in 1413, but the fortunes of the Stourton family reached their peak with his son, Sir John Stourton (d.1462), who was high in the favour of Henry VI. He was appointed to the Privy Council in 1437, and in 1439 was a member of the commission which treated for peace with the French king, Charles VII, having custody of the Duke of Orleans on that occasion. He became Treasurer of the royal household and was created Baron Stourton in 1448. He enlarged Stourton House, according to Leland building 'a goodly gate-house and front ... ex spoliis Gallorum' (with French prize-money). Licence was also

Old Stourton House from the south in 1685; from a sketch by John Aubrey

given him to enclose 1,000 acres of pasture, meadow and woodlands 'to impale and make thereof a park', and he received grants of land in support of his rank. In the time of his son William, the Stourtons owned property in Devon, Essex, Gloucestershire, Hampshire and Middlesex, although principally in Dorset, Somerset and Wiltshire.

Despite being a Catholic, the 6th Lord Stourton, whose effigy is in the church, was a member of that Parliament which supported Henry VIII in ending the Papal supremacy in England. His son benefited from the Dissolution of the Monasteries, acquiring the manor of Kilmington, which had belonged to Shaftesbury. But here began a story which precipitated the decline of the Stourton fortunes. The tenant of Kilmington under the monastery was a William Hartgill. William, 7th Lord Stourton was Deputy-General for the King at Newhaven, and in his absence he entrusted Hartgill with the management of his estates, and the care of his wife and children, who lived in Hartgill's house at Kilmington. Stourton House was occupied by a relative, William Fauntleroy. Meanwhile Lord Stourton was living at Newhaven with a daughter of the Countess of Bridgewater, Agnes Ryce, with whom he departed to France, where he died in 1548, having made Agnes a considerable bequest of his movable property at Stourton. The residue was left to his son, Charles, who became 8th Lord Stourton, but apparently the Dowager Lady Stourton, who continued to live at Kilmington, got nothing. Charles Stourton immediately dismissed Hartgill, who had already been accused of mismanaging his father's affairs. In a long and bitter feud between Lord Stourton and the Hartgills violence was done on both sides. Things came to a head in 1556 in a dispute over an allowance for maintenance of the Dowager Lady Stourton, who was still living at Kilmington. Lord Stourton's men took possession of Hartgill's house, forcing old Hartgill and his wife to take refuge in Kilmington church tower. The following August the justices at Frome gave judgement against Lord Stourton, who was committed to the Fleet Prison, but temporarily released to go and pay the damages awarded to the Hartgills. On the pretext of doing this, he met Hartgill and his son at Kilmington church, arrested them and took

The tomb effigies of Edward, 6th Lord Stourton (d.1536), and his wife, Agnes, in Stourton church; engraving from Sir Richard Colt Hoare's History of Modern Wiltshire, *1822*

them to his house at Bonham, where they were murdered in his presence. For this he and four of his men were hanged in Salisbury market place on 6 March 1557.

Although Lord Stourton's estates were forfeit to the Crown after his conviction, the family subsequently suffered more from being Catholic. John, 9th Lord Stourton was a child when his father met his death and was brought up by his mother. At his majority in 1573 he tried to escape abroad, but was arrested. After a short imprisonment he was entrusted to Matthew Parker, Archbishop of Canterbury, who brought about at least an outward show of conformity to the new religion. He died in his mid-thirties at Stourton in 1588, and as he had no children, the estates passed to his brother. Edward, the 10th baron, was one of the Catholic peers warned to be absent from Parliament on 5 November 1605, and thus came under suspicion of being privy to Guy Fawkes's plot. He was committed to the Tower, and released on the payment of a heavy fine. He was succeeded by his son William in 1633.

The 11th Lord Stourton supported the Royalist cause, but did not apparently bear arms. In September 1644 Stourton House was attacked by Parliamentary troops under Edmund Ludlow and rendered uninhabitable. The inmates escaped to Oxford, from where Lord Stourton wrote to Lord Grey of Warke in March 1646 asking for permission to go into Wiltshire and reside in any tenant's house, 'for all my estate is sequestered, and my wife, children, and grandchildren have not beds to lie on'. The request was denied, and the family was still in Oxford in 1648, under conditions which were becoming increasingly difficult for Catholics. The Test Act of 1673 excluded them from any office, civil or military; and following the scare of Popish plots, and concern that the throne should not pass to a Catholic monarch, they were excluded from both Houses of Parliament too. The 12th Lord Stourton was one of the peers so affected. He died in 1685 at the age of 40, leaving impoverished and encumbered estates. In 1688 Edward, the 13th baron, appears to have followed James II into exile. The heavily mortgaged Stourton estate was taken over by Sir Thomas Meres in 1714. Lord Stourton received £755 19s 9d after his debts had been discharged. He died in Paris in 1720, intestate and childless. His brother, Thomas Stourton, settled at Bonham, Stourton Manor having been bought by Henry Hoare, the second generation of the banking family.

THE HOARE FAMILY

SIR RICHARD HOARE
(1648–1718)

The founder of Hoare's Bank, Sir Richard Hoare was the son of a successful horse-dealer. At the age of seventeen he was apprenticed to a goldsmith, and by 1672 he was in business on his own at the sign of the Golden Bottle, Cheapside. He later moved to Fleet Street where the firm has flourished ever since. Throughout the seventeenth century the goldsmiths had been evolving a system of accepting money on trust and lending it at high rates of interest. They gave receipts, called 'goldsmiths' notes', for money deposited, and then promissory notes against which they guaranteed to pay. Thus arose the earliest form of banknote in England.

In order to meet the cost of the Dutch War and increasing Court extravagance, Charles II's government anticipated part of the annual revenue by borrowing from the goldsmiths. By 1672 it was in debt to such an extent that it had to stop payment of interest, thus precipitating a number of goldsmith-

(Right) Sir Richard Hoare, founder of Hoare's Bank; by Jonathan Richardson (Entrance Hall)

bankers into bankruptcy. Richard Hoare took over the goldsmith's business of his master, Robert Tempest, in 1673. He was associated with Francis Child and Charles Duncombe in opposing the foundation of the Bank of England, which they saw as a rival. Duncombe withdrew £80,000 in 1695, with which he bought the Helmsley estate in Yorkshire. His successors built a new mansion, calling it 'Duncombe', and, as at Stourhead, erected temples and made the famous terrace (now also the property of the National Trust) overlooking the ruins of Rievaulx Abbey. Richard Hoare prospered, and on Queen Anne's succession was knighted. He had represented the City of London in Parliament from 1709 to 1713, and was Lord Mayor in 1712. In the same year he became one of the original directors of the South Sea Company. The stock held by him and his sons yielded a handsome profit when speculation started in 1720, although Sir Richard did not live to see it, for he died in 1718.

He had eleven sons, not all of whom, as his letters show, practised the virtues of diligence and prudence on which his economic success depended. The eldest, Richard, from whom most of the present partners in Hoare's Bank are descended, was an import and export merchant, but his business was largely carried by his father, to whom at one time he owed £62,000. Only two sons became partners in the bank, Henry, his second son, and the youngest, Benjamin.

HENRY HOARE
(1677–1725)

Henry Hoare bought the manor of Stourton from Sir Thomas Meres's son John in 1717. At that time he already had a house in Quarley, near the Wiltshire border with Hampshire, and close to his cousin and brother-in-law, William Benson, at Newton Toney. In the eighteenth century, buying land was one of the few ways of investing surplus wealth, besides being the means of acquiring the political power which landowners possessed. The Hoare family, however, has always seen its business as the main source of its prosperity, and has clung to it tenaciously, resisting the takeovers which have absorbed other private banks. It is partly for this

reason that Stourhead is so well preserved. This was the name given to the house built by Henry Hoare I to replace the house of the Stourtons which he pulled down. In view of its sack in the Civil War, and the troubles subsequently endured by the Stourtons, it was probably uninhabitable.

Stourhead was one of the first country villas in the new Palladian style, thanks to William Benson, one of the promoters of the new fashion. Benson had secured the post of Surveyor-General in succession to Sir Christopher Wren, whose style was associated with the Tory regime of Queen Anne, whereas the Whigs, who came to power with George I, felt the need for a new national taste, to replace that of a single court architect 'with too much of the Gothick', as the Earl of Shaftesbury put it. The severely classical Palladian style of architecture had first been introduced into England by Inigo Jones in the reign of James I. Its revival in the second decade of the eighteenth century was stimulated by the publication in 1715 of the first volume of *Vitruvius Britannicus* by Colen Campbell, in which he gave examples. He also secured the interest and support of a wealthy patron and amateur architect, Richard Boyle, 3rd Earl of Burlington, who was, incidentally, a customer of Hoare's Bank. Colen Campbell became Deputy-Surveyor under Benson; so, all things considered, it is hardly surprising that he should be the architect of Stourhead, the designs for which were published in the third volume of his work in 1725. Henry Hoare died the same year, when the house was just completed. His widow, Jane Benson, lived there until her death in 1741.

HENRY HOARE 'THE MAGNIFICENT'
(1705–85)

Because so many of the Hoares were named 'Henry' or 'Richard', they have been distinguished within the family by nicknames. Henry Hoare I has been called 'Good' Henry because of his charitable works; his son, Henry Hoare II, whose great achievement was the creation of the famous land-scape garden with its lake and temples, is known as Henry 'the Magnificent'. The big equestrian portrait in the Entrance Hall shows him at the age of 21, just after his father's death, inheritor of a flourishing business, and recently married to Ann, daughter of Lord Masham. Her mother, Abigail Masham, as Keeper of the Privy Purse in 1710, had brought the account to Hoare's Bank. Unhappily, Ann died in childbirth, and just over a year later Henry married Susanna Colt, daughter and heiress of Stephen Colt of Clapham. According to what he later told his grandson, Richard Colt Hoare, Henry was accustomed in early manhood to a 'gay and dissolute style of life'. He was a good horseman and a good shot. Another early portrait, now in the Little Dining Room, shows him out hunting with his uncle Benjamin.

But there was another side to his character, probably influenced by his uncle Benson, who was well

(Left) Henry Hoare I, the builder of the house; by Michael Dahl (Entrance Hall)

Henry Hoare 'the Magnificent', creator of the gardens; by Michael Dahl and John Wootton (Entrance Hall)

known for his literary tastes and patronage of artists. Henry Hoare bought Benson's house at Wilbury, east of Amesbury, in 1734, and the same year he became MP for Salisbury. Nearby was Amesbury Abbey, where the poets Pope and Gay often visited the Duchess of Queensbury. Henry Hoare advised Gay on his investments and undoubtedly knew Pope. In fact, as a banker, he was at the centre of things. He lent money to William Kent, one of the leaders of the revolution in garden design; names like Vanbrugh, Carlisle and Burlington headed pages in the bank's ledgers. The more these noblemen improved their estates, the more they borrowed and the more the interest mounted. At the same time Henry Hoare acquired the habit 'of looking into books and the pursuit of that knowledge which distinguishes only the gentleman from the vulgar', as he put it. His letters abound in evidence that he was familiar with the works of Ovid and Virgil, Pope and Akenside, and there are plenty of biblical turns of phrase too. Indeed it is one of the fascinations of the man to see how the lover of pagan imagery is revealed as a deeply Protestant banker; how emotion is complemented by reason, almost as the 'natural' beauties of the landscape coexist with the severe lines of Palladian architecture. In all his enthusiastic pursuit of an ideal, he never forgot the realities behind it, writing in 1755:

Whether at pleasure or business let us be in earnest, and ever active to be outdone or exceeded by none, that is the way to thrive. ... What is there in creation [at Stourhead] ... those are the fruits of industry and application to business, and shows what great things may be done by it, the envy of the indolent, who have no claim to Temples, Grottos, Bridges, Rocks, Exotick Pines and Ice in Summer.

Henry Hoare did not move from Wilbury to Stourhead until after his mother's death in 1741. He was abroad from 1738 until that year. In 1743 his wife, Susanna, died, leaving him with a son of thirteen and two small girls of eleven and six. He did not marry again, and it was in these circumstances that he began the landscape garden which was one of his main preoccupations for the remainder of his life. The first was always the soundness of his business, and he divided his time between London and Wiltshire. His other concern was the future of his

family, and in this he was greatly saddened in that all his children predeceased him. His son, Henry, died in Naples at the age of 21. His younger daughter, Anne, married her cousin Richard, son of Henry Hoare's only brother. Their son was Richard Colt Hoare, who eventually became his grandfather's heir. Anne died in 1759, and Richard Hoare married Frances Acland of Holnicote, north Devon. Henry's elder daughter, Susanna, first married Charles Boyle, son of the Earl of Cork and Orrery, and after his death (also in 1759), Thomas, Lord Bruce of Tottenham, 1st Earl of Ailesbury. The proximity of Tottenham House in Savernake Forest to Stourhead made correspondence relatively easy. From 1760 onwards Henry wrote regularly to his son-in-law and daughter, announcing all his projects and recording the progress of the work, the pleasures of which he was able to share with her and his grandchildren.

When Henry Hoare took possession in 1741, he made alterations to his father's house, particularly

Sir Richard Hoare, 1st Bt, of Barn Elms; he married Henry Hoare's daughter, Anne, and their son, Richard Colt Hoare, inherited Stourhead; by Francis Cotes, 1757 (Little Dining Room)

the rebuilding of the west front to accommodate the Saloon, a big room with a coved ceiling, destroyed in the fire of 1902 and not restored in its original form. In all his architectural works he employed Henry Flitcroft, a protégé of Lord Burlington, who succeeded William Kent as Master Mason and Deputy-Surveyor, and finally became Comptroller of the Works in 1758. In the 1720s and early 1730s he had executed Lord Burlington's designs for Tottenham Park (eventually the home of Henry Hoare's son-in-law), and in 1729 he had given a design for Benjamin Hoare's house at Boreham in Essex. His most notable contributions to Stourhead were the temples round the lake and Alfred's Tower, but in 1753–4 he also designed a villa on the north side of Clapham Common, where Henry Hoare spent an increasing amount of time at the end of his life.

The patronage of the arts at Stourhead did not stop at architecture; painting and sculpture also had an important place. One of Henry Hoare's earliest purchases was the painting of *The Bloody-shouldered Arabian* by John Wootton, now in the South Apartment, but he started collecting in earnest during and after his visit to Italy. He bought works in English sales and through dealers in Paris and Rome, including Sir Horace Mann, who got him the big painting by Carlo Maratta, now in the Picture Gallery, and the two big landscapes by Gaspard Dughet. As a companion to the Maratta, Henry commissioned the painting of *Caesar and Cleopatra* by Anton Raphael Mengs, an early example of the Neo-classical taste in England. Among other paintings in his collection were two by Nicolas Poussin. *The Choice of Hercules* is still at Stourhead, but the important *Rape of the Sabines* was sold in 1883, and only details from it copied by Samuel Woodforde now remain as reminders of its former home.

Henry Hoare was a faithful patron of Michael Rysbrack, from whom in 1747 he commissioned the statue of *Hercules* in the Pantheon by the lake. The terracotta model in the Library was left to Henry Hoare by Rysbrack in his will. His last work for Stourhead is the bust of Alfred the Great in the Library Ante-Room. The painter William Hoare of Bath, whose pastels hang in the Little Dining

The Choice of Hercules; by Nicolas Poussin (Picture Gallery). One of Henry Hoare's most important surviving acquisitions for Stourhead

Room, was not a relation, but a regular visitor to Stourhead, as was the amateur painter, architect and landscape gardener Coplestone Warre Bampfylde, who lived at Hestercombe near Taunton. In fact after his daughters' marriages there was no mistress at Stourhead, whose management was conducted by a series of housekeepers. The society which assembled there seems to have been predominantly male. Colt Hoare spent his holidays there as a boy and recalled that the long winter evenings were passed in a 'constant game of piquet'. Henry Hoare, he wrote, was 'tall and elegant in his person, elegant in his manner and address'. At the age of 76, although his hands were rheumatic, he was still able to ride over to Savernake and climb the scaffold of a column being erected to inspect the dripstone. But, what with the Gordon Riots (particularly violent in the neighbourhood of Fleet Street) and the loss of the American colonies, he became increasingly pessimistic, and in this mood he decided that his grandson, Richard Colt Hoare, should immediately inherit. As he put it, 'he had seen for some time past the progress of this nation's ruin'; by securing Colt an estate of £6,000 a year with a fine house and place, on condition that he left the banking business, Stourhead would be preserved 'let any public calamity happen'. In his state the place was more pain than pleasure to him; he would resign it to Colt, finishing the remainder of his days at Clapham, living on his income from business and free from care and vexation. He executed deeds in August 1783 leaving the bank premises and his London house in Lincoln's Inn Fields to his nephew Richard (Colt Hoare's father), and his West Country estates to Colt, who was married that year. He died at Clapham in September 1785, having outlived his daughter Susanna by about a year.

SIR RICHARD COLT HOARE
2nd Bt (1758–1838)

Samuel Woodforde, who painted the large portrait of Colt Hoare and his son which is in the Entrance Hall, said that 'Sir Richard...was a shy man to strangers, but liberal and steady in his attachments'. His devotion to scholarship was in keeping with his conscientious, industrious, even meticulous nature. Henry Hoare imposed a classical vision on the countryside; Colt Hoare sought to possess the past by painstakingly recording it. The sober announcement at the head of his *Ancient History of Wiltshire*, 'We speak from facts not theory', is typical of the man and of the times in which he lived. The Library at Stourhead is his characteristic creation.

Colt Hoare grew up in his father's house at Barn Elms in Surrey with a family of half-brothers and half-sister. As Henry Hoare's favourite grandchild, he frequently visited Stourhead in childhood and saw the building of the Temple of Apollo, the arrival of the Bristol Cross and the rise of Alfred's Tower. After private schools at Wandsworth and Greenford, he entered the bank, and while learning the business continued to study classics under a tutor. In 1783 he married Hester Lyttelton of Hagley (where there was another famous Palladian house and landscape garden), and went to live at Stourhead, having given up his connection with the bank as his grandfather requested. Hester gave birth to a son in the

year following her marriage, but died in 1785 after a second pregnancy. Colt Hoare was so distressed that he left Stourhead in charge of a steward and travelled the Continent. Except briefly in 1787, he did not return for six years.

Most of the time was spent in Italy, a period of residence rather than a Grand Tour. At first his inclination was towards painting – before leaving England he took lessons from John 'Warwick' Smith. In the first part of his life he was a prolific if uninspired artist, and his work is of interest as a topographical record, particularly of Italy and Wales, as the handwritten and illustrated volumes of his travels in the Library at Stourhead testify. Engravings after his drawings illustrated his friend William Coxe's *Historical Tour in Monmouthshire* and his own translation of Giraldus de Barri's *Itinerary of Archbishop Baldwin through Wales, AD 1188*. While in Rome he sought the company of artists, and conceived a great admiration for the very large watercolour paintings of the Swiss artist Louis Ducros, many of which, representing scenes visited by Colt Hoare in Italy, remain at Stourhead. Colt Hoare always maintained that he influenced the course of watercolour painting in England by introducing Turner, Francis Nicholson and others to Ducros's work. He commissioned Turner, then a young man at the beginning of his career, to paint a series of large watercolours of Salisbury. Turner also made an oil painting of *Lake Avernus with Aeneas and the Cumaean Sibyl* after one of Colt Hoare's drawings. An early version is in the Tate Gallery; a later version, formerly one of the glories of the Stourhead collection, is now in the United States. His most important purchase from Italy was the big *Adoration of the Magi* by Cigoli, in the Picture Gallery. He was a faithful patron of Samuel Woodforde, RA, who as a young man had been assisted both by Henry Hoare and Colt Hoare's father. And he bought paintings by other English Royal Academicians: typical of his rather sentimental taste are the two by Henry Thomson, *Distress by Sea* and *Distress by Land*, which were shown in the Royal Academy exhibitions of 1804 and 1811 respec-

(Right) Sir Richard Colt Hoare, 2nd Bt, and his son, Henry; by Samuel Woodforde (Entrance Hall)

The Library in 1808;
watercolour by
Francis Nicholson
(Library)

tively. On the other hand his strong interest in topography led not only to the Turner pictures, but also to commissions to John Buckler for records of Wiltshire churches and houses, and the magnificent series of views of Stourhead made about 1813 by Francis Nicholson, most of which are in the British Museum.

This aspect of his patronage complemented his work as an antiquary and historian, on which his enduring reputation depends, particularly the recording of the prehistoric remains of Wiltshire, which he undertook with William Cunnington between 1803 and 1810. This was the extension of an interest first aroused in Italy by the civilisation of the Etruscans, but brought to an end by events on the Continent which for many years confined Englishmen within their island. From the edge of the chalk scarp opposite his house an unrivalled group of prehistoric monuments extended across Salisbury Plain and the Marlborough Downs, to which his attention was now turned, resulting in the publication of the two volumes of *The Ancient History of Wiltshire*. These were followed by the thirteen volumes of *The History of Modern Wiltshire* by a number of authors (including himself), whose

work he co-ordinated and encouraged, and whose rallying point was the Library he had built to house his outstanding collection of topographical books and printed records. This fine room was furnished by the younger Chippendale; indeed the furniture made by him for Stourhead between 1795 and 1820 is among the most notable achievements of the Regency cabinetmaker's art, and is preserved in almost perfect condition.

Outside the house Colt Hoare also left his mark. He built ten lodges. The entrance drive is due to him; formerly it went through the stableyard, which was probably the site of one of the court-yards of Stourton House, the medieval gateway of which was taken down and rebuilt in its present position. He removed all traces of regularity in the grounds south of the house, and in the 1790s and early 1800s introduced new varieties of trees, mainly broad-leaved. Planting round the lake included the introduction of *Rhododendron ponticum* in 1791, and later two *R. arboreum*. He set a pattern for walks, laying down gravel paths and making an entrance near the village. Otherwise he respected his grand-father's creation, except to remove some smaller buildings on the hillside near the house 'to render the design of the gardens as chaste and correct as possible, and to give them the character of an Italian villa'. In 1809 he started cultivating geraniums, and by 1821 he had some 600 varieties. There are many references to him in Robert Sweet's *Geraniaceae* (1820–2).

In many ways Colt Hoare seems to have been a lonely man; even more than in his grandfather's day, Stourhead saw little female company. Colt Hoare had been an indefatigable traveller for most of his life, first abroad, then in search of British antiquities. He spent much time in Wales, where he had a house near Bala and a lasting friendship with the historian of Pembrokeshire, Richard Fenton. But he ceased to go there after Fenton's death in

Maria Acland, wife of Sir Henry Hugh Hoare, 3rd Bt, with their son, Hugh Richard; by Samuel Woodforde

1821, and during the last years of his life he suffered increasingly from deafness, gout and rheumatism. The entries in his diaries became fewer, dwindling in 1832 to three, beginning 'still house-bound, deaf and lame'. On 18 April 1836, he wrote: 'Spring day. Out after a confinement of five months'. His life ended at a quarter to six on the morning of 19 May 1838.

SIR HENRY HUGH HOARE
3rd Bt (1762–1841)

Colt Hoare left his estates in tail male; that is to say in succession to the nearest male relative so that they could not be disposed of by anyone as absolute owner. His only son, Henry, having died two years previously, his immediate heir was his half-brother, Henry Hugh Hoare, who became the 3rd Baronet. They had been close since childhood and had common interests, both being elected Fellows of the Society of Antiquaries. Henry Hugh was a partner in the bank; thus Fleet Street and Stourhead were once more united. During the three years left to him he added a portico to the house according to Colen Campbell's original intention. He also took down the Obelisk, erected by Henry Hoare in 1746–7, and rebuilt it in Bath stone. He died at Wavendon in Buckinghamshire, an estate bought by his father, the 1st Baronet. He was succeeded by his son, Hugh Richard Hoare. Except in the case of Henry Hoare II, this was the only occasion on which Stourhead descended from father to son.

SIR HUGH RICHARD HOARE
4th Bt (1787–1857)

The 4th Baronet was then 54, and had been a partner for twelve years. In 1845 he retired to Stourhead with an annual allowance from the business of £5,200, increased in 1852 to £8,000. This income undoubtedly helped him to devote resources to the estates, which on Colt Hoare's death amounted to some 11,000 acres (4,689 in Wiltshire, 3,781 in Somerset, 2,791 in Dorset), and included about 50 farms. The Stourhead Annals, a record of building and planting instituted by Colt Hoare, show the yearly improvement to farm buildings on all the

Sir Hugh Richard Hoare, 4th Bt

estates (farmhouses, cottages, barns, cattle-sheds and wagon-houses), with a wide substitution of tile roofs for thatch. In 1846 an entry notes that the Hartgills' old dilapidated house at Kilmington was taken down, and a cowstall erected near the site. With a practical concern for the future he planted many trees, adding new species of conifer, including specimens of Douglas Fir and Western Hemlock in the Pleasure Grounds. His lack of children meant that the succession went to his nephew, Henry Ainslie Hoare, son of his brother, Henry Charles, who had died in 1852.

SIR HENRY AINSLIE HOARE
5th Bt (1824–94)

The 5th Baronet was educated at Eton and Cambridge. He entered the bank, and in 1845 married Augusta Frances East, daughter of Sir East George Clayton East. They spent the first part of their honeymoon at Stourhead where, in later life, Augusta was to experience the happiest times of a relatively unhappy life. She was essentially a woman of firm family attachments, first to her mother, then to her daughter Augusta ('Gussy'), and finally to her four grandchildren, whom she virtually brought up. Henry Ainslie, on the other hand, had a restless temperament which looked for satisfaction in a varied and active social life, in the excitements of hunting and the racecourse, and in politics. It was gambling that began Augusta's real troubles, for an influential client of the bank drew the attention of the partners to Henry Ainslie's habits, as a result of which he was dismissed in 1848, being later given an allowance. In June he left for France, a country to which he had a lifelong attachment. Augusta followed in October with their two children, Gussy, born in December 1845, and Charles, born in September 1846.

The latter died and was buried at Neuilly shortly before his ninth birthday, thus once again breaking the direct succession at Stourhead. The news of the 4th Baronet's death reached Paris on 11 January 1857. Henry and Augusta returned to England in June and arrived at Stourhead on the 13th, remaining till late October, when they returned to France. This pattern of summer and autumn in Wiltshire, alternating with winter and spring in London or abroad, continued for 28 years, at least for Augusta, who came to regard Stourhead as home. The portrait of her, on the left of the great equestrian picture of Henry the Magnificent in the Entrance Hall, was painted in Paris in 1858 by Frederic Leighton, then 28. He began it in January, shortly after she had written in her journal at the end of 1857, 'Another year full of pain and a little pleasure'. Leighton remained a close friend until his death in 1896. His portrait of Gussy (on the window wall of the Saloon) was painted in London when she was fourteen and a half. Her unhappy life was another continuing cause of distress to her mother, but, ironically, it contributed to Augusta's happiness, in that she was closely concerned with bringing up Gussy's four children, who regularly went to Wiltshire in the summer. Accounts of rides round the gardens or the woods in donkey-chairs and wagonettes, picnics at the Convent or Alfred's Tower and parties with the village children in the Picture Gallery are a cheering picture of this part of the Stourhead story.

Henry Ainslie came to Stourhead to hunt or shoot. The management of the estate was in the hands of his steward, Robert Shackleton, whose daily journals from 1863 to 1887 show that it was not neglected during that time. Entertaining was lavish in the London houses Sir Henry and his wife inhabited at different times. One of the functions at Stourhead, so far as he was concerned, was to send fresh vegetables to town. Although Sir Henry and his wife led virtually independent social lives, he always came home to be nursed when ill, which he often was with gout. Indeed it was one of Augusta's continual occupations to sit with the sick and dying, whether they were relations, servants or people in the village, for the picture that emerges in her journals is of a genuinely devout person, with a real concern for others. And, in a different way, this was not entirely untrue of Henry Ainslie. As Liberal MP for New Windsor from July 1865 to April 1866, and for Chelsea from 1868 to 1874, he spoke cogently

Augusta East, wife of the 5th Baronet; by her friend, Lord Leighton (Entrance Hall)

Sir Henry Ainslie Hoare, 5th Bt; by J. P. Knight, 1860 (Entrance Hall)

from a consistent liberal point of view, with an awareness of the problems of his poorer constituents. But he was also greatly interested in foreign affairs, and his longest speeches and strongest feelings were against England's failure to support France in the Franco-Prussian war of 1870–1.

The sale of the Stourhead Heirlooms in 1883 was a great loss to the collections in the house but, as the preamble to the Act of Parliament required to break the Trusts set up under Colt Hoare's will explains, agricultural depression had reduced the annual rental of the farms to the extent that there was insufficient income for their maintenance. The proceeds of the sale were to go to paying off a mortgage created by Colt Hoare's executors. Every item to be sold had to be approved by the heir, Sir Henry Ainslie's cousin, Henry Hugh Arthur Hoare (or rather by his guardians, for he was a minor). Among the greatest losses were Turner's *Lake Avernus* and his series of watercolour paintings of Salisbury, Nicolas Poussin's *Rape of the Sabines* and (from Stourhead's point of view) Francis Nicholson's pictures of the grounds (now in the British Museum). Even more sad, perhaps, was the dispersal of Colt Hoare's unique library of books on British history and topography.

In 1885 Sir Henry Ainslie contested East Somerset as a Tory, having left the Liberal Party on the issue of Free Trade. He was defeated in this traditional Hobhouse seat, and left Stourhead after polling day. Two days later Augusta followed him to London, noting in her journal afterwards, 'How little I thought I was leaving my beloved home forever'. Sir Henry said his income was insufficient to allow him to live in the mansion or to keep the gardens in suitable order. The fact is that Henry Hoare's creation was expensive to maintain, and for this reason there was difficulty in finding a tenant for the house. So Stourhead was shut up. Sir Henry continued to spend much of his time in France. He was taken gravely ill at Nice in January 1894, but recovered sufficiently to struggle to Paris on 9 May, finally reaching London, where he died at his home in Eaton Place on 7 July. He was buried at Stourton. Augusta lived ten years more.

Sir Henry Hoare, 6th Bt, who restored the house after the fire and gave it to the National Trust; by St George Hare (Entrance Hall)

HENRY HUGH ARTHUR HOARE
6th Bt (1865–1947)

The 6th Baronet had no direct interest in the bank at any time. His father died when he was eight and his early life was spent with his mother at Wavendon, where he lived after his marriage to Alda Weston in 1887. Their only son was born on 30 July 1888. Sir Henry was still only 29 when he moved to Stourhead, and he was not a stranger to the place, as he had managed the woodland for his cousin since 1891. The estate was not in a bad condition generally; a large sum had been laid out in drainage, and it was well let at a time when many landlords with far greater resources had tenants giving up their farms and the poorer lands going out of cultivation. On the other hand the Pleasure Grounds were overgrown, and the house had been untenanted for seven years. While this was being put in order, Sir

Henry and his wife lived in what they called 'The Cottage' (the present National Trust office), which had been converted for their use. They moved to the house in 1897. Thus began the longest continuous occupation in Stourhead's history. For 53 years they gave it their undivided attention; its almost miraculous survival of a disastrous fire and two world wars is due to them.

The 6th Baronet, more than any previous owner, lived the life of a country gentleman. Although he became a director of Lloyds Bank, and went to London regularly for meetings, his main interest was in country matters, particularly horses, where his expertise in judging was often called for. His breed of Percherons (a strong, fast breed of draught-horses derived from French post-horses) was famous. By consent, outside the house was his domain, while the inside of the house was controlled by his wife, Alda. She was a woman of decided tastes and opinions which she did not hesitate to express, and she was given to dismissing her employees summarily for 'misbehaviour'. Whereas Sir Henry hardly ever changed a servant, she had a reputation for having a near-permanent advertisement in the local press. She did not on the whole enjoy the company of women, and quoted with approval Swift's remark, 'I never knew a tolerable woman to be fond of her own sex'. Nor did she like Society. All her emotional nature, dominance and possessiveness were directed to her husband, son and Stourhead. From the first her personality was brought to bear on the interior, which was rearranged to her taste, furniture from Wavendon mixed with Colt Hoare's Chippendale without regard to the place for which it was originally intended. The result can be seen in photographs taken in 1901. The Library, Picture Gallery and other downstairs rooms were furnished for 'living', and Alda Hoare gave variety to life by moving what she called her 'headquarters' from one to the other at different times of the year. She had a strong interest in literary men, and read much in both French and English. Among those with whom she had a personal acquaintance were the historian and biographer Charles Whibley, a tenant of Wavendon and friend, and Thomas Hardy, whose first editions are in the Library. She carried on a long correspondence with Hardy's second wife, Florence.

It is certainly Alda Hoare's taste which resulted in the patronage of the painter St George Hare. Apart from the portraits of herself and Sir Henry painted in 1907, now in the Entrance Hall, and a three-quarter-length picture of Lady Hoare holding a Malacca cane (1910), he supplied a number of fancy pictures with titles like *The Angel's Love, Cupid sharpening his arrow on the twenty-fifth mile-stone* and *The Gilded Cage*. Another favourite was the landscape painter Yeend King, whose Academy picture of 1910, *Stourhead in Spring: 'there is a quiet spirit in these woods,'* had a very great success.

A fire in 1902 gutted the central part of the house, with the loss of all the furniture in the upper floors. Most of the furniture and pictures on the ground floor were saved, and the Library and Picture Gallery were untouched. Sir Henry was at a Lloyds Bank meeting in Salisbury at the time. He had a

Alda, Lady Hoare; by St George Hare (Entrance Hall)

special train chartered back to Gillingham, where a pony and trap were waiting. He made the pony gallop all the way to Stourhead. After this the family moved into 'The Cottage', remaining there until 1904. The reconstruction of the house proceeded remarkably quickly, first under Doran Webb of Salisbury, and then (after he proved unsatisfactory) under Sir Aston Webb (no relation) and his son Maurice. By July 1904 the Hoares were able to return to rooms in the south wing; the restoration was complete in 1907.

A far more shattering blow was the death of their only son in 1917. Henry Colt Arthur Hoare had been born at Wavendon in 1888. He was educated at Harrow, and while still at school had been seriously ill with heart trouble. He went to Trinity College, Cambridge, and after graduating in 1910 became his father's agent for all the estates. The properties were as extensive as in Colt Hoare's day and also included Wavendon and Oxenham. Between 1910 and 1918 most of the outlying properties in Dorset, Somerset and Wiltshire were sold, reducing the holdings by some 5,000 acres. Oxenham went in 1911, and Wavendon finally in 1919, not before some of the valuable chimneypieces had been moved to Stourhead to replace those lost in the fire. On the outbreak of war in 1914, Harry (as his mother called him) joined the Dorset Yeomanry, which suffered heavy losses at Gallipoli in 1915. During the evacuation of the Dardanelles in December, he was in charge of a machine-gun section. He became critically ill with double pneumonia and typhoid, and returned to hospital in England. He last saw Stourhead in 1916 while convalescing from February to May, and for ten days in July on overseas leave. On rejoining his regiment he fought in Palestine and was shot through the lungs in the attack on Mughair Ridge. He died at Rassellin Hospital, Alexandria, and was buried in the Hadra Military Cemetery.

His parents were naturally grief-stricken. Alda Hoare never recovered. She preserved his room exactly as he had left it; his favourite walk in The Shades, his portrait, everything at Stourhead served to keep his memory alive. By 1938, with the approach of another world war, Sir Henry had decided to give the house and gardens to the National Trust, with sufficient land to support them. Stourhead's continuing existence was largely due to him; apart from rebuilding the house, he planted extensively. In the Pleasure Grounds he introduced many new varieties of tree, especially conifers. Between 1925 and 1938 he replaced *Rhododendron ponticum* with many kinds of Himalayan hybrid.

The gift of some 3,000 acres to the National Trust was made in 1946, the remaining 2,215 acres were bequeathed to Sir Henry's cousin, Henry Peregrine Rennie Hoare, the eldest son in the direct male line of Sir Richard Hoare, the founder of the bank, and a descendant through the female line of 'Good' Henry, who built Stourhead. The 6th Baronet died on Lady Day 1947. Alda Hoare had constantly expressed the fear that she would be left alone; it might almost have been her last determined act of will to die six hours later.

Harry Hoare in 1909; by St George Hare (Saloon)

THE HOARES OF STOURHEAD

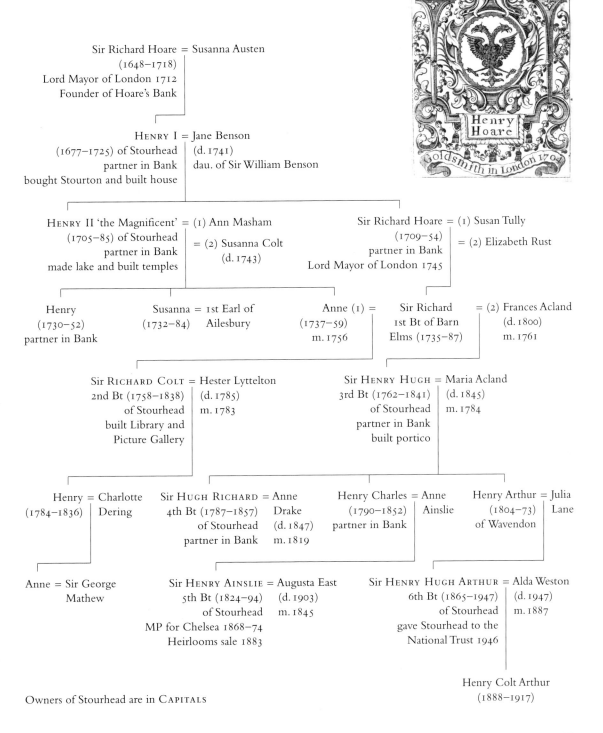

Sir Richard Hoare = Susanna Austen
(1648–1718)
Lord Mayor of London 1712
Founder of Hoare's Bank

Henry I = Jane Benson
(1677–1725) of Stourhead | (d. 1741)
partner in Bank | dau. of Sir William Benson
bought Stourton and built house

Henry II 'the Magnificent' = (1) Ann Masham
(1705–85) of Stourhead
partner in Bank | = (2) Susanna Colt
made lake and built temples | (d. 1743)

Sir Richard Hoare = (1) Susan Tully
(1709–54)
partner in Bank | = (2) Elizabeth Rust
Lord Mayor of London 1745

Henry | Susanna = 1st Earl of | Anne (1) = | Sir Richard | = (2) Frances Acland
(1730–52) | (1732–84) Ailesbury | (1737–59) | 1st Bt of Barn | (d. 1800)
partner in Bank | | m. 1756 | Elms (1735–87) | m. 1761

Sir Richard Colt = Hester Lyttelton
2nd Bt (1758–1838) | (d. 1785)
of Stourhead | m. 1783
built Library and
Picture Gallery

Sir Henry Hugh = Maria Acland
3rd Bt (1762–1841) | (d. 1845)
of Stourhead | m. 1784
partner in Bank
built portico

Henry = Charlotte | Sir Hugh Richard = Anne | Henry Charles = Anne | Henry Arthur = Julia
(1784–1836) Dering | 4th Bt (1787–1857) Drake | (1790–1852) Ainslie | (1804–73) Lane
| | of Stourhead (d. 1847) | partner in Bank | of Wavendon
| | partner in Bank m. 1819

Anne = Sir George | Sir Henry Ainslie = Augusta East | Sir Henry Hugh Arthur = Alda Weston
Mathew | 5th Bt (1824–94) (d. 1903) | 6th Bt (1865–1947) | (d. 1947)
| of Stourhead m. 1845 | of Stourhead | m. 1887
| MP for Chelsea 1868–74 | gave Stourhead to the
| Heirlooms sale 1883 | National Trust 1946

Owners of Stourhead are in Capitals

Henry Colt Arthur
(1888–1917)

47

BIBLIOGRAPHY

ALMA, Roger, 'Thomas Hardy and Stourhead', *National Trust Studies*, 1979, pp. 99–111.

AVERY, Charles, 'Hubert Le Sueur's Portraits of King Charles I in Bronze, at Stourhead, Ickworth, and elsewhere', *National Trust Studies*, 1979, pp. 128–47.

BRITTON, John, *The Beauties of Wiltshire*, 1801.

CLIFFORD, Timothy, 'Cigoli's Adoration of the Magi at Stourhead', *National Trust Year Book*, 1997–8, pp. 1–17.

CONFORTI, Michael, 'Pierre Legros and the Rôle of Sculptors as Designers in late Baroque Rome', *Burlington Magazine*, August 1977.

CORNFORTH, John, 'Stourhead, Wiltshire', *Country Life*, 8 September 1994, pp. 64–7.

DODD, Dudley, 'Rebuilding Stourhead 1902–1906', *National Trust Studies*, 1979, pp. 113–27.

EUSTACE, Katherine, *Michael Rysbrack, Sculptor 1694–1770*, Bristol Museum and Art Gallery, 1982.

[FENTON, Richard], *A Tour in search of Genealogy*, 1811.

GORE, St John, 'Prince of Georgian Collectors' and 'A Worthy Heir to Greatness', *Country Life*, 30 January, 6 February 1964, pp. 210–12, 278–80.

HAYWARD, Helena, and KIRKHAM, Pat, *William and John Linnell, Eighteenth Century London Furniture Makers*, London, 1980.

HOARE, H. P. R., *Hoare's Bank: A Record 1672–1955*, London, 1955, and *Hoare's Bank at the Sign of the Golden Bottle*, London, 1975.

[HOARE, Richard Colt], *A Description of the House and Gardens at Stourhead*, 1800, 1818 [guidebook].

[HOARE, Richard Colt], *The History of Modern Wiltshire: The Hundred of Mere*, 1822.

HUSSEY, Christopher, 'Stourhead, Wiltshire', *Country Life*, 11, 18 June 1938, 5 January 1951.

JOURDAIN, Margaret, 'Furniture at Stourhead, Wiltshire', *Apollo*, July 1948.

KENWORTHY-BROWNE, John, 'Notes on the Furniture by Thomas Chippendale the Younger at Stourhead', *National Trust Year Book*, 1975–6, pp. 93–102.

KENWORTHY-BROWNE, John, 'Portrait Busts by Rysbrack', *National Trust Studies*, 1980, pp. 66–79.

KENWORTHY-BROWNE, John, 'Rysbrack, *Hercules* and Pietro da Cortona', *Burlington Magazine*, April 1983.

LAING, Alastair, *In Trust for the Nation*, London, 1995, pp. 38–9, 160–1, 198, 216, 237–8.

LEES-MILNE, James, *Stourhead, Wiltshire*, London, 1948 [guidebook].

LEES-MILNE, James, *Ancestral Voices*, London, 1975.

LEES-MILNE, James, *People and Places*, London, 1992, pp. 68–83.

MOWBRAY, SEGRAVE AND STOURTON, Charles, Lord, *The History of the Noble House of Stourton*, privately printed, 1899.

NEWBY, Evelyn, *William Hoare of Bath RA, 1707–1792*, Victoria Art Gallery, Bath, 1990.

NICOLSON, Benedict, 'Caravaggesque Pictures in National Trust Houses', *National Trust Year Book*, 1975–6, pp. 1–7.

POCOCKE, Richard, *Travels through England*, 1754; J. J. Cartright, ed., 1889.

POWYS, Mrs Lybbe, *Passages from the Diaries of Mrs Lybbe Powys*, E. J. Climenson, ed., 1889.

RUSSELL, Francis, 'The Stourhead Batoni and other Copies after Reni', *National Trust Year Book*, 1975–6, pp. 109–111

STAINTON, Lindsay, *Images of the Grand Tour: Louis Ducros, 1748–1810*, Iveagh Bequest, Kenwood, London, 1985.

STUTCHBURY, Howard E., *The Architecture of Colen Campbell*, Manchester, 1968.

SWEETMAN, George, *Stourhead Mansion*, editions from 1885 [guidebook].

WALPOLE, Horace, 'Journal of Visits to Country Seats', *Walpole Society*, xvi, 1927–8, pp. 41–3 [visit in 1762].

WEBB, Michael E., *Michael Rysbrack, Sculptor*, London, 1954.

WILTON, Andrew, and BIGNAMINI, Ilaria, ed., *Grand Tour: The Lure of Italy in the Eighteenth Century*, Tate Gallery, London, 1996, pp. 278, 294–7.

WOODBRIDGE, Kenneth, *Landscape and Antiquity*, Oxford, 1970.

WOODBRIDGE, Kenneth, *The Stourhead Landscape*, London, 1971.